Art Masterpieces of
FLORENCE

Designed and Produced by

...RT
and
DAVID GIBBON

COOMBE BOOKS

INTRODUCTION

From the Middle Ages Florence has been an important centre of art, science and political thought. Her history, however, dates back to c. 187 BC, when the Roman town of Florentia was built at the foot of a hill on which stood the Etruscan town of Faesulae, now known as Fiesole. The name, Florentia, meaning 'flourishing town', was probably chosen as an augury and, indeed, the town did flourish and become an important centre, as roads from east to west and north to south, along the Arno Valley, were extended through the city, although commerce, craftsmanship and an abundant supply of water were also contributory factors to her growth.

In the years that followed, invasion by the Goths, and later by the Byzantines and Lombards, reduced the Roman amphitheatre, temples, baths and other buildings to piles of rubble. It was the great Charlemagne, who visited the city no less than three times, to whom legend accords responsibility for the reconstruction of Florence in the 8th century. The medieval city was built on a level from four to ten feet above the ancient remains and it included many fine churches.

In 1052 Florence, together with the rest of Tuscany passed into the hands of Countess Matilda and, under her influence, progressed towards political and administrative autonomy. The city, however, had grave internal problems in the form of conflicts between the Guelphs and the Ghibellines. The Florentine people, the Guelphs, were loyal to the Popes, and the Ghibellines to the Emperors. As one party won so it would exile the other, who would lose no time in seeking assistance from outside in order to recover power. It was during this time that an exiled Ghibelline from Florence, Dante Alighieri, chose the more vulgar speech of Tuscany in which to write his epic work 'The Divine Comedy', and in so doing made Tuscan the literary language of Sicily.

In 1250 the city was proclaimed a republic and after ten years of Guelph supremacy Florence became not only one of the chief cites of Italy but one of the most influential in civilized Europe.

From 1434 her history was intertwined with the rich and powerful Medicis – a family of bankers. Cosimo de' Medici was a great benefactor of literature and the arts and a friend of other Italian and European rulers. He was succeeded by his son Piero the Gouty, whose reign was brief and undistinguished. Lorenzo the Magnificent, who followed Piero, was a poet of considerable talent and, like his grandfather, a wise politician and a patron of the arts. It was under his rule that Florence was adorned with great artistic works and became the centre of European culture. His son Giovanni became Pope Leo X and another Medici, Francesco I, was responsible for founding the world famous Uffizi Gallery. Ferdinand I, his brother, under whom Florence attained even greater heights of power and prosperity, was next to rule but his successors, alas, were responsible for the city's decline and the eventual transference of power to the House of Lorraine.

Francesco was the Lorraine's first Duke of Tuscany. He was, however, married to Maria Teresa of Austria and preferred to live in Vienna where, in 1745, he received the crown of the Hapsburg Empire. From 1765-1790, Tuscany came under the competent rule of Pietro Leopoldo but he too was summoned to assume the crown of Austria. His son Ferdinand III was left to govern but he was weak and before long he was expelled by French forces and the Duchy was ruled successively by Ludovico I of Parma and Elisa Baciocchi, the sister of Napoleon. With the death of the French Emperor, Ferdinand III returned to Tuscany to regain his dukedom and for a time the region enjoyed relative peace under him and his son Leopold II.

However, during a wave of nationalism in the middle of the nineteenth century, Leopold II was driven out, and in 1860 Tuscany proclaimed itself part of the kingdom of Italy – of which Florence became the capital from 1865-1871.

Perhaps the next most significant happening in the history of Florence was during the summer of 1944. World War II had reduced much of the Tuscany coast to a battlefield. Sadly for Florence German troops blew up all her bridges except the Ponte Vecchio, as well as many of the medieval buildings along the Arno River. After they had retreated rebuilding began in earnest.

Another tragedy occurred in 1966 when terrible floods, believed to be worse than those of 1333 and 1557, caused immense and costly damage, both to buildings and to art treasures. In some places water rose to a depth of nearly twenty feet, leaving everywhere deposits of mud and debris, as well as oil from central heating systems. The Uffizi Gallery and the Pitti Palace escaped but many churches and their contents suffered badly. International aid poured into the city and this, together with the rugged determination of the Florentines, enabled much of the damage to be rectified. Restoration still continues but all the museums and monuments have now reopened – to be admired by countless visitors from all over the world.

In her fine buildings Florence displays the genius of architects like Brunelleschi, Giotto, Alberti and Buonotalenti, and inside them may be seen the outstanding work of such masters as Ghirlandaio, Titian, Botticelli, Fra Angelico, Michelangelo and Leonardo da Vinci.

The whole of Florence may fairly be described as one magnificent treasure house. The Uffizi Gallery has collections of incalculable value which include major works from all the Italian and other European Schools. The Pitti Palace, built in the middle of the fifteenth century, has over five hundred paintings beautifully displayed and the Academy contains Michelangelo's renowned sculpture 'David' as just one of its exhibits.

The rest of Florence's great buildings are too numerous to describe fully in the space available here. Only a visit to this unique city can fully reveal the splendour of her heritage or, failing that, a book such as this, which lays before the reader many of the glories of Florence.

The magnificent statue of David, in the Gallery of the Academy *left*, is the work of **Michelangelo** Buonarroti (c. 1475-1564).

The historic buildings of the beautiful city of
Florence cluster around the Cathedral of Santa Maria
del Fiore, the third largest church in the world, and
although work began on the cathedral in 1296, it was
not completed until the end of the 19th century.
Towering regally over the red-tiled roofs *above* is the
cupola, Brunelleschi's masterpiece, whilst *above right*
the magnificent façade, faced with coloured marble,
blends harmoniously with the Baptistry *far right*. Built
on the site of an old, early Christian Basilica, the
octagonal plan of the Baptistry, with geometric
marble patterns, is an outstanding example of
Romanesque architecture. Of the three gilt-bronze
doors, the most splendid is the East door, known as
the Gate of Paradise. This masterpiece of
Renaissance art represents, in ten panels, scenes from
the Old Testament, and took Lorenzo **Ghiberti**
(c. 1378-1455), with the help of his sons, twenty seven
years to complete.

The scene of the city's major historical events, the
Piazza Della Signoria *right*, is dominated by the
Palazzo Vecchio with its elegant tower and mullioned
windows.

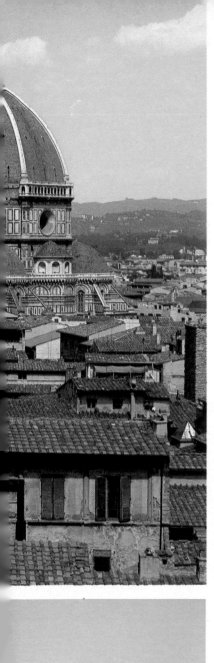

The East door of the Baptistry is illustrated *above*, revealing the extent of Ghiberti's craftsmanship and *right* is shown in detail the panel representing the meeting between Solomon and the Queen of Sheba.

Also the work of **Ghiberti**, the North door *above right* is similar to that of Pisano's South door, in that both are divided into twenty-eight panels. Executed in 1425, with the help of some of his pupils who included Donatello and Uccello, the panels depict scenes from the New Testament, Doctors of the Church and the lives of the Evangelists.

Situated in the last chapel of the left transept of the Santa Maria del Fiore Cathedral is **Michelangelo's** emotive study, the 'Pietà' *left*. It is thought that the artist intended to have the sculpture placed on his own tomb, but the work was unfinished at the time of his death and completed by Tiberio Calcagni, who added the figure of Mary Magdalene. Nevertheless, the dramatic, rhythmic lines created by the continuous intertwining of the bodies, convey the deep sense of emotion in the theme of the 'Descent from the Cross'.

In the church of Santa Maria Novella, the apse of the main chapel is covered with a series of frescoes including the detail *above left* from 'Herod's Feast and the Dance of Salome' by Domenico **Ghirlandaio** (c. 1449-1494): featured in the Spanish chapel is 'The Triumph of St Thomas Aquinas' *left* by **Andrea da Firenze** (c. 1337-1377).

Within the Church of Santa Croce are many outstanding works of art, amongst them the magnificent Tomb of Michelangelo, and the painting *above*, 'The Doubting Thomas' by Giorgio **Vasari** (c. 1511-1574).

The Laurentian Library *above*, designed by **Michelangelo** for Pope Clement VII, houses a rare collection of priceless manuscripts, including the famous Virgil of the 4th or 5th centuries, and about 100 codices of Dante.

The Brancacci chapel, within the Carmine Church, contains a cycle of frescoes begun in 1424–5 by **Masolino** da Panicale (c. 1384–1447) and completed by his pupil, **Masaccio** (c. 1401–1428), who painted 'The Expulsion of Adam and Eve from Paradise' *above right*. Also included in the fifteen frescoes are 'The Temptation of Adam and Eve' *above far right* and 'St Peter raises Tabitha from the Dead' *right*, executed conjointly by Masolino and Masaccio.

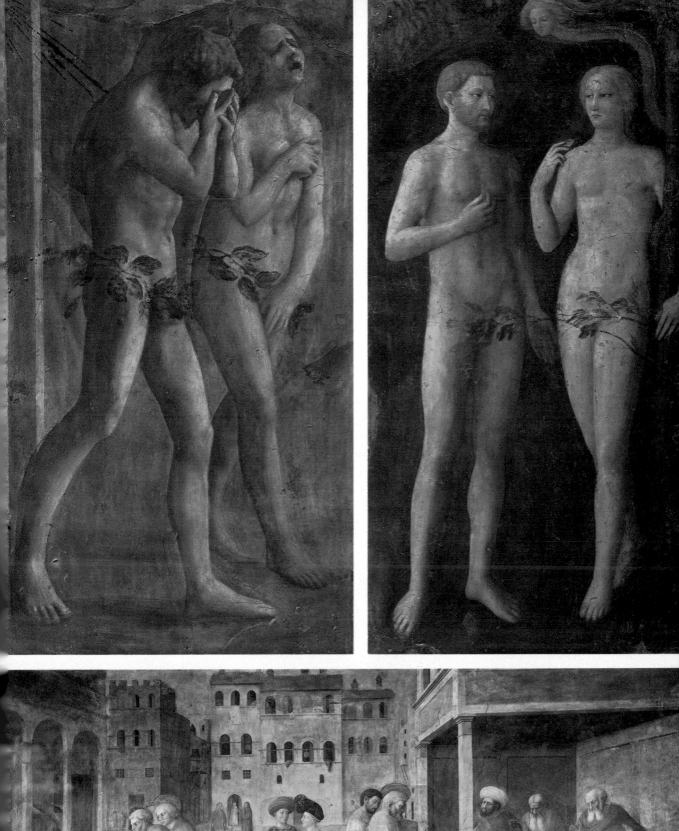

The Museum of San Marco is housed in an ancient 13th century convent, on the site of an old monastery of the Vallombrosian monks. Rebuilt in 1437, by Michelozzo, to the order of Cosimo the Elder, the Convent was taken over by the Dominican Order and **Fra Angelico** (Guido di Pietro) (about 1400-1455), with the help of a number of assistants, was responsible for the decoration of the cells and common rooms.

After the suppression of the monastic order, in 1866, the Convent was converted to a museum and devoted to Fra Angelico, who adopted the name of Fra Giovanni da Fiesole when he became a Dominican monk, some time between 1420 and 1422. The early Renaissance Florentine style of this deeply religious artist reveals his innate gentleness and sensitivity, and because of his angelic virtues, gave rise, after his death, to the name of Angelico.

The compassionate compositions, by Fra Angelico, illustrated on these pages, sombre in both theme and colour, portray with deep intensity the sufferings of Christ.

'Christ Mocked' is shown *above left*, 'The Crucifixion' *below left*, 'The Descent from the Cross' *right* and *below* 'Christ at the Gates of Hell'.

These further works exemplify
Angelico's mastery. The detail *right*
depicts the grieving Madonna
'Lamenting the Dead Christ', and t
sublime facial expressions are
indicative of the artist's deep
emotional intensity.

Throughout his life Angelico
combined the pious monastic life
continued activity as a painter, and
although the majority of his work
consists of the murals executed in
Convent of San Marco, he also
worked in Rome, decorating the
chapel of Pope Nicholas V, in the
Vatican.

On his return to Florence, he was
responsible for producing a cycle
thirty-five paintings for the door
silver chest, which includes the
familiar theme of 'The Last Suppe
illustrated *above*, and *left* is shown
'Judas receiving Payment' for his
betrayal of Christ. On the first floo
the Convent can be seen the old
Dominican cells with the frescoes
painted, for the most part, by Ang
and his pupils; and in the Prior's
Quarters is sited the double cell,
numbered 32-33, which is believe
be the one occupied by Angelico
during his attachment to the Con

Within the Pilgrims' Hostel, which is sited to the right of the San Marco Museum entrance, are numerous paintings on wood which reveal Fra Angelico's development as an artist. Amongst the finest is 'The Last Judgement', details of which are shown *above, left and overleaf.*

The upper section *left* depicts Christ enthroned, surrounded by a heavenly host of angels, pronouncing his final judgement on mankind. The right-hand section, illustrated *overleaf* portrays the condemned descending into hell's inferno, whilst the left-hand section, pictured *above,* denotes the righteous joining with the angels in a jubilant dance.

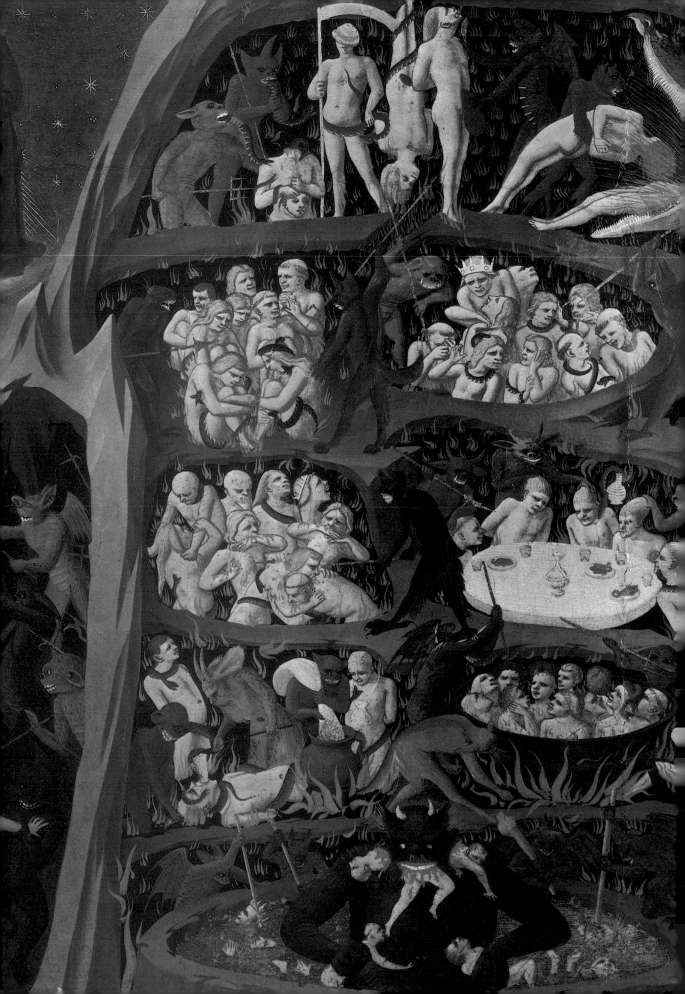

Leading from a small door off the hall on the first floor of the Palazzo Vecchio, also known as the Palazzo della Signoria or del Popolo, is the Study of Francesco I, exquisitely decorated by Giorgio **Vasari** (c. 1511-1574), and known as 'Il Tesoretto' (the Little Treasury), as it originally served as the Duke's strong-room.

The Gallery of the Academy contains not only a superb picture gallery, but also some of Michelangelo's most important sculptures. The 'Palestrina Pietà' *left*, although unfinished, remains one of the artist's most significant and moving works; the barely outlined faces conveying pathos and anguish in this scene of great drama.

Behind the Church of San Lorenzo are the magnificent Medici Chapels, which can also be reached from the interior of the Church. In the New Sacristy, so called to distinguish it from the Old Sacristy (the work of Brunelleschi), are the tombs of the Medici princes, the great rulers of Florence. Begun by Michelangelo in 1520 and completed by Vasari in 1557 the spacious interior is linked by pilaster strips and blind windows, and the emphasised outlines of 'pietra serena'.

The beautifully sculpted head of Giuliano, Duke of Nemours, by Michelangelo, is illustrated *right* and adorning the sarcophagus beneath the sculpture are two figures representing Day and Night, a detail of which is shown *above right*. Michelangelo has continued the theme on the sarcophagus of the tomb of Lorenzo, Duke of Urbino, with the figures denoting Dawn and Dusk, a detail of which is shown *above*.

The Museum of the Opera del Duomo, at the rear of the Cathedral, contains relics from the Cathedral, the Baptistry and the Campanile and architectural remains from earlier buildings on the site. In the 'Room of the Choir Galleries' can be seen many important sculptures, including **Donatello's** (c. 1386–1466) 'Jeremiah' *left*.

Within the 'Room of the Panels' are some of the panels carved by Andrea **Pisano** (c. 1270-90-1348–9) for the Campanile. The carving *below* represents the art of building and *below left* the medical practitioner. Also incorporated is the panel *above*, portraying the poet Orpheus and *above left* the pupils receiving instruction in Latin grammar.

The origins of the Church of San Lorenzo can be traced as far back as AD 393 when it was consecrated by S Ambroso, Bishop of Milan. The Church has undergone several majo transformations, having been rebuilt in the Romanesque style in the 11th century, and later altered by Brunelleschi at the request of the Medici family, first in 1419 and again between 1442 and 1446. It was finally completed by Antonio Manetti, in 1460, except for the reconstruction of the façade, which was to have been carried out by Michelangelo. Michelangelo did, however, add the Laurentian Library and the New Sacristy, in the right arm of the transcept, which complements Brunelleschi's Old Sacristy; the latter being sited in the left arm.

In the centre aisle, on each side of th altar, are two pulpits executed by **Donatello** with the aid of his pupils. and which date from about 1460. Constructed of bronze and wood the pulpits, the exquisite detailing of which can be seen *above*, show the artists' superb craftsmanship and depict scenes from the 'Passion of Christ'. The panel *above right* portray the emotional scene of 'Christ's Descent from the Cross' and illustrat *left* is 'Christ brought before Pilate'.

The magnificent Silver Reredos in the Museum of the Opera del Duomo is a superb example of Florentine gold-smiths' art of the 14th and 15th centuries. The intricate detailing on the altar screen depicts scenes from the life of St John the Baptist and *below* is illustrated a section of the screen portraying the meeting between Christ and the Prophet.

Construction on the famous Uffizi Palace *far right* began in 1560, to the plan of Giorgio **Vasari** (c. 1511-1574), for Cosimo I de' Medici. The original idea of the building was to provide administrative headquarters for Florence, but after the death of Cosimo, the offices were sited in the Palazzo Vecchio and the new Grand Duke was able, therefore, to utilize the Uffizi for the Medici art collections; so began the magnificent Gallery which now contains the greatest of Italian treasures as well as foreign art. The whole building, which extends from the Arno River to the Palazzo Vecchio, is of local grey stone on white plaster and the famous 'Vasariano' corridor links the Gallery to the Pitti Palace. The marble-floored 'Third Corridor' *above* is lined with beautiful tapestries, and sculptures of the 3rd and 4th centuries BC. Commencing the Gallery's impressive collection of paintings, illustrated here and on the following eighteen pages are:–

'Madonna and Child with Angels and Prophets' *right*, by **Cimabue** (Cenni di Pepi) (before 1251-1302), an important work by this great Tuscan painter. 'Madonna and Child with Angels and Saints' *left*, by **Giotto** (di Bondone) (about 1267-1337) was originally painted for the High Altar of the Ognissanti Church.

One of the most sensitive exponents of Gothic art, Simone **Martini** (c. 1284-1344), did much to spread the influence of Sienese painting, and his work is imbued with pure, harmonious colour and a gracefulness of line. The triptych *above left*, 'The Annunciation' was painted in collaboration with his brother-in-law, Lippo **Memmi** (c. 1285-1361), for the Cathedral of Siena.

Gentile da Fabriano (G. di Nicolo di Giovanni Massi) (c. 1370-1450) executed the altarpiece, 'Adoration of the Magi', a detail of which is shown *left*, for the Strozzi Chapel in Santa Trinità, Florence. His work exemplifies the splendour of the Florid International Gothic style and this magnificent example is considered to be the artist's masterpiece.

The 'Coronation of the Virgin' *above* further illustrates the outstanding qualities of the art of **Fra Angelico**. Painted for the main Florentine Hospital of Santa Maria Nuova, the composition reveals his deep mysticism and combines both Gothic and Renaissance characteristics.

The 'Baptism of Christ' *left*, although attributed to the great sculptor Andrea del **Verrochio** (c. 1435–1488), reveals, as in much of his painting, the collaboration of other artists. It is believed that Leonardo, when an apprentice to Verrochio, contributed the angel in profile and the majority of the landscape.

The portraits of 'Federigo di Montefeltro' *below* and his wife 'Battista Sforza' *above* are the work of **Piero della Francesca** (c. 1420–1492) and denote the subtle and disciplined art of this important Italian Renaissance artist.

'The Ascension' *right* is part of a triptych by the first Renaissance artist of northern Italy, Andrea **Mantegna** (c. 1431?–1506); the other two panels depicting 'The Adoration of the Magi' and 'Circumcision'.

One of the greatest exponents of early Florentine Renaissance art, Sandro **Botticelli** (c. 1445-1510), trained under Fra Filippo Lippi and by 1470 had established his own atelier in Florence. Patronised by the powerful Medici family, Botticelli's career was highly successful and financially rewarding. Included in the Gallery's extensive collection of his paintings is the world-famous 'Birth of Venus' *left*, which like 'Primavera' ('Allegory of Spring') *above left*, embodies the spirit of the renascent era. Botticelli painted 'Adoration of the Kings' *above* for the Lami Chapel in Santa Maria Novella, Florence, and several notable members of the Medici family are depicted in the composition, including Lorenzo the Magnificent and Cosimo the Elder.

Pietro **Perugino** (c. 1450-1523) is noted for his religious paintings and 'Madonna and Child between St John the Baptist and St Sebastian' *right* is a typical example of the artist's work.

'The Annuciation' *right* and the unfinished painting of 'The Adoration of the Magi' *above right* are the work of **Leonardo** da Vinci (c. 1452-1519), a man of genius who excelled not only in the field of painting, developing his masterly technique of a superb atmospheric blending of light and shade, known as 'sfumato', but also in the spheres of sculpture, architecture and engineering. His drawings show his acute perception of the anatomy of the human body, whilst his scientific explorations reveal the brilliance that was centuries ahead of his time.

Luca **Signorelli** (c. 1445/50-1523), a Renaissance painter primarily known for his nudes and innovative compositional inventiveness, was strongly influenced by Florentine naturalism and in particular by the Pollaiuoli brothers. 'The Crucifix and Saints' *above*, portraying the SS Jerome, Francis and John the Baptist, the Blessed Colombini and Mary Magdalene, was painted in collaboration with **Perugino.**

Fra Filippo **Lippi** (c. 1406-1469) joined the Carmelite Order, in 1421, at Sta Maria del Carmine in Florence during the time that Masaccio was working on the frescoes in the Brancacci Chapel and his early work shows the influence of this outstanding artist. A highly gifted painter, Lippi also spent a considerable amount of time in Prato where he was responsible for the decoration of the Cathedral choir, and it was during this period that he was released from his vows in order to marry Lucrezia Buti, who gave birth to a son, Filippino, in 1457.

Included in the Gallery's wide collection of his paintings are the three superb examples illustrated on these pages.

'Madonna and Child with Two Angels' *left* is a particularly delightful study, enhanced by the gentle, ethereal beauty of the Madonna and typical of Renaissance art of the period, whilst the 'Adoration of the Infant Jesus with St Hilarius' *right* and 'Coronation of the Virgin' *above* reveal Lippi's intricate detailing and splendid use of colour.

Michelangelo Buonarroti (c. 1475–1564), like
Leonardo, was one of the greatest and most
versatile artists of the Renaissance, whose
scope encompassed sculpture, painting,
architecture and poetry. The magnificent
'Doni Tondo' *left* of 'The Holy Family' was
painted on the occasion of the marriage
between Agnolo Doni and Maddalena Strozzi.

'Rest on the Flight into Egypt' *right* is an early
work by Antonio Allegri **Correggio**
(c. 1494–1534) a Renaissance artist of the
Parma school. Influenced by Raphael and
Michelangelo, Correggio's paintings are
remarkable for his harmonious use of colour
and unified compositions.

The work of Lorenzo **Lotto** (c. 1480–1556) is
characterised by his perceptive portraiture
and mystical paintings of religious subjects.
'A Holy Conversation' *below* is a mature
composition and depicts the Holy Family
with the Saints Jerome and Anne.

One of the first of **Raphael** Santi's (c. 1483-1520) famed series of Madonna altarpanels 'The Madonna of the Goldfinch' is illustrated *left* and reveals his growing mastery of Leonardo's innovative 'sfumato' technique. The son of the painter Giovanni Santi, Raphael's early apprenticeship was to the Perugino, from where he moved first to Siena and then on to Florence, studying the works of the masters of the early Renaissance and Michelangelo and Leonardo. Ranked amongst the greatest of the Italian High Renaissance artists, Raphael is admired for his graceful compositions and skilful application of the art of perspective.

'Portrait of Leo X with the Cardinals Giulio de' Medici and Luigi de' Rossi' *above* is one of his later works and displays the formal grandeur and rich attire of the powerful church hierarchy.

Rosso Fiorentino (Giovanni Battista di Jacopo) (c. 1495–1540) was one of the founders of the Fontainebleau school, and his most highly regarded work is considered to be the decoration of the Galerie François I at the palace of Fontainebleau. 'A Putto Musician' *above* is a delightful painting by this influential artist and denotes the emotionalism of the Mannerist style.

Agnolo **Bronzino** (c. 1503–1572), a noted painter of the sophisticated Florentine Mannerist style, is particularly renowned for his portraiture which displays the impersonal, reserved poses favoured by the Medici, by whom he was employed as Court Painter. Initially influenced by Pontormo and to some extent by Michelangelo, he created his own precise style, developing a rich use of colour and high degree of finish. One of a pair of panel portraits 'Lucrezia Panciatichi' *right* is a companion study to that of her husband Bartolomeo, and illustrated *left* is 'Portrait of a Princess of the Medici family'.

Influential in the development of
Baroque painting, **Caravaggio**
(Michelangelo Merisi) (c. 1573-1610)
used the highly contrasted effects of
light and shadow, known as tenebris
to add drama to the realism of his
paintings. 'The Youthful Bacchus'
above left is an early composition by
the artist, whose work was both
revolutionary and original.

Generally regarded as the greatest
German Renaissance artist, Albrech
Dürer (c. 1471-1528), was also an
accomplished printmaker. 'Madonna
and Child' *above* is one of his many
paintings on religious themes.

'Flora' *right* and 'The Urbino Venus'
left are indicative of the mastery of
Titian (Tiziano Vecellio) (c. 1488/9
1576), whose skill in oil painting and
brilliant use of colour place him
among the finest artists of the
Renaissance, and one of the outstan
ing figures of Western art.

The magnificent Pitti Palace was built to the plan of **Brunelleschi** by Luca **Pancelli** in 1458, for the Florentine banker Luca Pitti, who jealously challenged the supremacy of the Medici. Condemned to death for his actions, he was, however, reprieved and the Palace was purchased by Cosimo I.

Within the Palace is the splendid Palatine Gallery, housing a large collection of works of art, including 'The Young Bacchus' *right*, the work of Guido **Reni** (c. 1575-1642). The collection was started by Cosimo II, in 1620, and constantly enlarged by the Medici family and later by the House of Lorraine.

The exquisite Room of the Saturn *above*, named after the frescoes on the ceiling, executed by Ciro **Ferri** (c. 1634-1689), contains works by many outstanding artists, including Raphael, Perugino and Andrea del Sarto.

The Green Room *left*, noted for its superb Gobelin tapestries depicting Stories of Esther, is one of a suite of rooms, the former royal apartments, which were once reserved for the use of the Kings of Italy.

The paintings illustrated on these pages are further exhibits from the Uffizi Gallery.

'Madonna Enthroned between two Angels' *left* is an outstanding example of the work of the Flemish artist Hans **Memling** (c. 1430/35-1494), the leading painter of the Bruges school.

'Portrait of Marie Zefferina of France' *above*, the daughter of Louis XV, is characteristic of the style of the artist, Jean-Marc **Nattier** (c. 1685-1766), a celebrated portraitist of the period and particularly noted for his studies of court ladies in classical dress.

Formerly attributed to Holbein the impressive full-length portrait of 'François I of France' *right* is by François **Clouet** (c. 1515/20-1572), an eminent painter of the Valois Court.

Included in the Palatine Gallery's collection of art masterpieces are **Titian's** 'Maddalena' *above*, and the 'Madonna of the Conception' *right* which denotes the depth of feeling and superb craftsmanship of the great Venetian Mannerist Painter Jacopo **Tintoretto** (c.1518-1594). Tintoretto received a vast number of commissions, including the re-decoration of the Palace of the Doge, which he executed in collaboration with Veronese, after the earlier frescoes had been destroyed in the fire of 1577. An indefatigable worker, he maintained a large workshop where he was assisted by his daughter, Marietta and his sons Mario and Domenico.

The soft and gentle art of **Raphael** is further exemplified by the beautiful study of 'Madonna of the Grand Duke' *left*, displayed in the Palatine Gallery's Room of Saturn and by 'The Woman with a Veil' *above*, considered to be a portrait of the Fornarina and exhibited in the Room of Jupiter.

Within the Palatine Gallery is a room devoted to the allegorical paintings of Baldassare Franceschini **Volterrano** (c. 1611-1689), and his canvas depicting 'The Joke of the Parish Priest, Arlotto' is illustrated *left*.

'Judith and Holofernes' *right* is displayed in the Room of the Education of Jupiter. The work of Cristofani **Allori** (c. 1577-1621), a painter of the late Florentine Mannerist school, the composition is considered to be the artist's masterpiece.

The romantic landscape paintings of Salvator **Rosa** (c. 1615-1673) exerted a profound influence on 18th century English nature painters. The graceful accomplishments of this skilled artist encompassed those of poetry, music and acting: a gifted etcher, Rosa was also successful in producing a number of prints. 'The Broken Bridge' *above* is a superb example of his work

The majority of the works of Bartolomé Esteban **Murillo** (c. 1618-1682) consist largely of religious themes and 'Madonna and Child' *left*, displayed in the Palatine Gallery's Room of Mars, is an exquisite example of his artistry.

The Room of the Iliad, with its splendidly decorated ceiling, contains the portrait of 'Waldemar Christian of Denmark' *right*, by the Flemish portrait and figure painter Justus **Sustermans** (c. 1597-1681), who spent the majority of his working life in Florence.

'The Consequences of War' *above* is one of the many mythological compositions by Peter Paul **Rubens** (c. 1577-1640); characteristic of the artist's dynamic energy, it embodies the sensuous exuberance of Baroque art, of which Rubens is considered to be the chief exponent.

Further paintings from the Gallery of the Pitti Palace are illustrated on this page.

'Madonna and Child' *above left* is the work of Carlo **Dolci** (c. 1616–1681) and characteristic of the artist's devotional paintings, executed with tender beauty and subtle colouring. A popular painter of his period, Dolci remained in Tuscany where he developed his style in the local Florentine Baroque tradition.

The portrait of 'Eleonora de' Medici' *above* is indicative of the ornate, grandiose style of the celebrated portraitist Frans **Pourbus** (c. 1569–1622). Employed at the Court of Mantua, Pourbus produced many studies of the nobility, including the Medici family and his paintings display the exquisite, ostentatious clothes of the era.

'The Three Fates' *left* is by Cecchino **Salviati** (Francesco de' Rossi) (c. 1510–1563), a pupil of Andrea del Sarto and one of the foremost Mannerist fresco painters of the Florentine-Roman school. This talented artist undertook a variety of ecclesiastical commissions, which he executed in Rome, Florence, Bologna and Venice, and among his most noteworthy frescoes are those painted for the Sala delle Udienza in the Palazzo Vecchio.

The intricately detailed composition *right*, 'The Golden Age', is the work of Jacopo **Zucchi** (c. 1541–1589/90), which is exhibited in the Uffizi Gallery.

Also included in the collection at the Pitti Palace are the following paintings:-

'Portrait of Musicians' *left* by Antonio Domenico **Gabbiani** (c. 1652-1726) who worked with Sustermans at his studio in Venice, and on his return to Florence established a highly successful Academy.

'A View of the Coast of Naples from the Sea' *above right* and 'The Convent of S. Paolo at Albano' *centre right* are both fine works by th artist and draughtsman, Gaspar van **Wittel** (c. 1653-1736), who was known in Italy as **Vanvitelli**.

'Naval Battle' *bottom right* is the work of Willem van de **Velde**, a noted painter of marine subjects.

Among the exhibits in the Museum Firenze Com'era, which houses a collection of engravings and drawings showing the development of Florence throughout the ag is the painting *below* depicting the 'Piazza Santa Croce during a Carnival' by Giovann **Signorini** (c. 1450-1523).

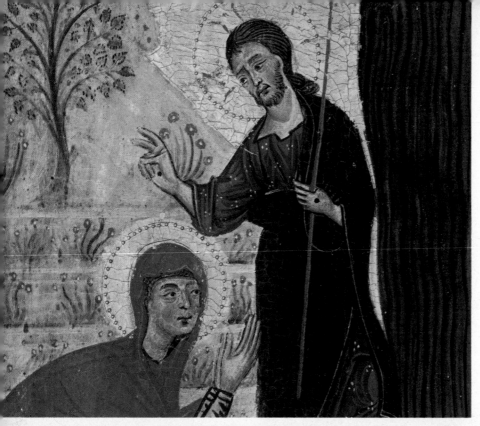

Within the Medici–Riccardi Palace, the official residence of the Medici up to the time of Cosimo I, is displayed the beautifully detailed painting *below*, 'Voyage of the Three Kings', the work of Benozzo **Gozzoli** (c. 1420-1497). The scene depicts the most notable personalities of the day, including Lorenzo the Magnificent and accurately records the costumes of the period.

The National Museum of the Bargello, housed in the Podesta Palace, contains a comprehensive collection of Italian decorative art and sculpture, including the composition of the Tuscan school of the 13th century, shown *left*, depicting 'Mary Magdalene'. **Michelangelo**'s superb tondo of the 'Madonna and Child' *right* is exhibited in the Chamber of the Council General, which is devoted to Donatello and other sculptors of the 15th century, whilst in the 13th Room, containing sculptures by Pollaiolo and Verrocchio, is Andrea del **Verrocchio**'s (c. 1435-1488) magnificent bronze statue of 'David' illustrated *overleaf*.

First published in Great Britain 1979 by Colour Library International Ltd.
© Illustrations: Foto Scala, Florence, Italy.
Colour separations by FERCROM, Barcelona, Spain.
Display and text filmsetting by Focus Photoset, London, England.
Printed by Cayfosa and bound by Eurobinder - Barcelona (Spain)
ISBN 0 904681 85 8

FOR MAX, BJÖRN, FREJ
& CHARLOTTE –
ROMAN RUIN EXPLORERS

Researched on location at Hadrian's Wall.
Historical consultant: Philip N Wood, Archaeologist.
Find out more about this book at
www.mickandbrita.com

No living creatures were harmed during the making of this book.

Roman Fort copyright © Frances Lincoln Limited 2004
Text and illustrations copyright © Mick Manning and Brita Granström 2004

First published in Great Britain in 2004 by
Frances Lincoln Children's Books, 4 Torriano Mews,
Torriano Avenue, London NW5 2RZ

www.franceslincoln.com

Distributed in the USA by Publishers Group West

British Library Cataloguing in Publication Data available on request

ISBN 1-84507-050-X

Printed in Singapore

1 3 5 7 9 8 6 4 2

ROMAN FORT

MICK MANNING & BRITA GRANSTRÖM

CONTENTS

FRANCES LINCOLN
CHILDREN'S BOOKS

WHO WERE THE ROMANS?

The Romans came from Italy and their capital city was Rome. They were clever people with new ideas about law, art, building and technology. With their mighty army and strong leaders, they invaded and conquered many countries and built a Roman Empire that would last from around 146 BC to AD 476. Some people welcomed Roman rule, but many fought against it until they were beaten by the Romans in battle.

Hadrian's Wall in northern England and the Raetien border in Germany are two famous frontiers and they form part of a network of forts and towns that covered the whole Roman Empire. The Romans had well-organized supply lines, and the people who lived under Roman rule had to provide money, food, gold, silver and slaves. Roman armies were stationed all over the frontier to make sure they did!

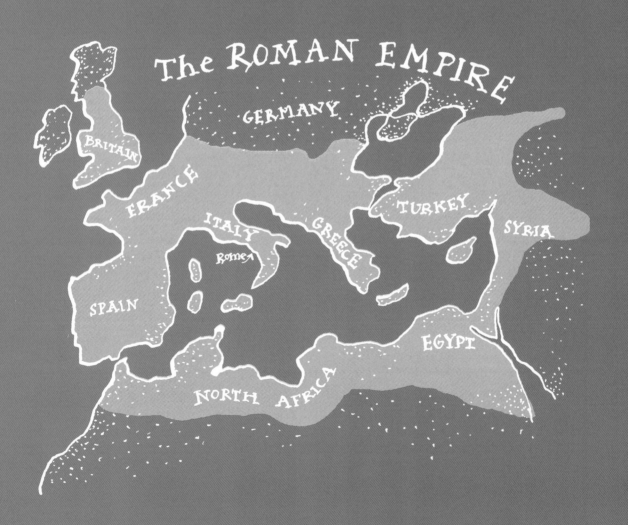

The ROMAN EMPIRE

BRITAIN
GERMANY
FRANCE
ITALY
Rome
SPAIN
GREECE
TURKEY
SYRIA
NORTH AFRICA
EGYPT

OUR FORT

The Roman fort in this sketchbook is on the northern frontier, far away from the city of Rome. Let's meet some of the people and look in on their lives.

Vespian
a centurion

Flavinus
a standard bearer

Candidus
a decurion

Felix
the fort commander

Claudia and Max
Felix's wife and their son

Lepidina and Titus
Claudia's best friend and her son

Marcus
a slave

Emperor Severus
the ruler of the Empire

Queen Meg
a local Celtic queen.

Claudia is having a birthday party and she has invited her best friend Lepidina. But Lepidina lives twenty dangerous miles away so Vespian has been sent to bring her safely to the fort...

It's raining cats and dogs!

Listen! Jangle, tramp! Jangle, tramp!
As the soldiers march, the sound of their metal belts mixes with the tramp of their studded boots.

Lepidina and Claudia write to each other but haven't met for months. 20 miles is a long way to travel in this wild country...

• A centurion like Vespian was in charge of a unit of 80 men called a century.

• Each century had a second-in-command called an optio, a trumpeter and standard bearers. Six centuries made a cohort and often included cavalry.

Flavinus, the standard bearer, holds the standard high.

Vespian is leading the troop back to the fort. On the way he must visit a powerful queen.

Flavinus also looks after his century's wages.

ON PATROL

Vespian's patrol is escorting Lepidina over the mountains. Roman troops must keep the Empire in order, even here in this rainy place somewhere on the northern frontier.

A 2000-year-old party invitation from a Roman lady called Claudia is the earliest surviving example of women's handwriting.

• Written with ink on birchwood, it was one of many letters dug up in the ruins of Vindolanda, a Roman fort in Northumberland, England.

WARRIOR QUEEN

Meg is a powerful Celtic queen. Some Celts still hate the Romans but Meg realised long ago that trade with the Empire could make her tribe rich. Vespian has a nickname for her – The Wild Cat!

Celtic houses are made of stones or woven branches covered with mud. The roofs are thatched with grass or reeds.

Enemy heads on poles to bring good luck!

The queen's daughters are full of mischief!

• The Celtic people of the northern frontiers lived in small villages. Each village was part of a larger tribe with its own king or queen.

• The Romans called the tribes 'barbarians' but the Cel made beautiful jewellery and used money, soap and perfume.

Inside it's smoky and dark – but very cosy!

The queen has never seen a peacock before! She is giving Vespian a puppy in return.

Sharp sticks are used to guard the village.

He smells of soap

Bleached hair

Tattoos and plant dye body paint

warm clothes in bright colours

He smells of ferrets!

'Arrow' will soon grow into a fast, hairy hunting dog.

To keep the peace, the Romans traded and gave many gifts from their Empire, including fine pottery, silver and peacocks.

• A famous Celtic queen called Boudicca burned London and massacred hundreds of people in revenge for attacks on her own family by Roman soldiers.

Oxen bring stone from the quarry.

'Creak' go the oxcart wheels.

Milestones mark distances between places.

Assistants hold up marker poles for Quintus.

"It's sweaty work!"

Some soldiers work - others stand guard.

The road is higher in the middle so any rain runs off into the ditches to avoid flooding.

• Romans used metal shovels, just like the ones you can find today in any hardware store.

• Roman engineers also built bridges and aqueducts. A fine example of a Roman aqueduct is at Pont Du Gard in France.

ROAD BUILDERS

Vespian's patrol has met up with Quintus and his road builders. Quintus loves building straight roads. The army can march quickly and easily from place to place, making it safer for everyone.

stubborn mules carry things too!

Quintus the surveyor decides which way the road should go. He plots the road across the countryside using an instrument called a 'groma'!

The Roman Road RECIPE:
① Dig a deep trench
② Fill it with broken stone and sand well packed down
③ Lay cobbles, paving stones or gravel on top.

What's that far-away sound?
strange trumpets... coming closer

By mixing broken tiles and small stones with cement, Romans made strong concrete. Concrete is still used by modern builders!

• Roads were kept as straight as possible but they did bend around burial grounds and holy places because the Romans were superstitious.

• Skeletons of Celts and Romans have been found showing tell-tale signs of battle injuries.

• Romans could stitch wounds, mend broken bones and even do amputations. But sickness and infection were the biggest killers.

AMBUSH!

This ambush could have led to disaster for
Lepidina. Vespian's men are outnumbered.
Luckily Candidus rides to the rescue.
What a hero! Celtic prisoners will face death,
slavery or life as Roman soldiers.

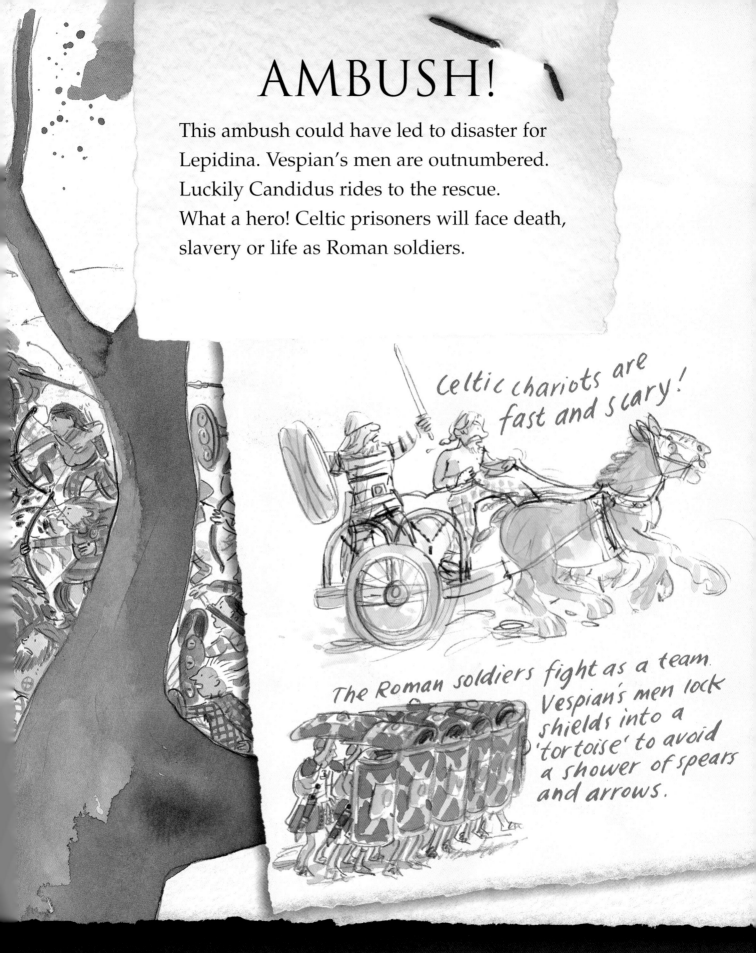

Celtic chariots are fast and scary!

The Roman soldiers fight as a team.
Vespian's men lock shields into a
'tortoise' to avoid a shower of spears
and arrows.

The Roman army was not always victorious.
In AD 9 three whole legions were wiped out
by fierce German tribes.

• Celts fought with spears, slingshots, bows and swords.
They had fast war chariots too.

AT THE FORT

Max likes to climb the hill. He can see the whole fort from up here: soldiers on parade, supplies arriving and being unloaded. Max's home is a very busy place!

Prisoners from the ambush ↓

Vespian's patrol is giving the password to open the gate. →

The headquarters is the nerve centre of the fort. The offices, strongroom and regiment flags and trophies are kept here.

The fort commander's house is large and even has a garden and private bathroom.

A watch-tower

The granary can hold enough food to feed 500 people for many months.

Max is waving to Vespian's patrol. He will see his friend Titus soon. It's windy today!

• Roman forts were built in the same shape as a playing card, with round corners. The very first forts were made of wood but later they were built of stone.

• The granary was where grain and other food supplies were stored. It was built on stilts to allow fresh air to circulate and to keep out the mice.

West gate

Fort commander's house

Headquarters

Hospital

Granary and food store

Cavalry patrol

vespian's quarters

vicus or settlement

Bar

shops

Bath house

Centurions and decurions had their own quarters
t the end of each barrack block. The cavalry soldiers
ften shared with their horses!

• The main gate's stone doorsteps were heavily worn
by iron cartwheels. These deep ruts still exist today
at many Roman fort ruins.

Rebels prefer life as a soldier to slavery – who wouldn't?

"Haircut"

"You pay for your own kit so look after it!"

"Sign up for a life in the army."

Too small?

Too big!

"Chain-mail is heavy but it can save your life!"

The senior centurion growls at the new recruits...

"You'll earn a good pay now that Rome is your mother. But you must learn to fight like a Roman too."

There are two sorts of Roman soldiers. Vespian's legionaries are Roman citizens but tribesmen who volunteer usually join as auxiliaries.

• Medics, clerks, musicians and craftsmen were excused from the boring jobs the soldiers had to do – things like cleaning the bath house or polishing armour.

• The soldiers' daily ration of food was about 1½ kgs (3 lbs) of bread, 1 kg (2¼ lbs) of meat, 1 litre (4½ cups) of wine and 400 millilitres (1½ cups) of olive oil.

18

A SOLDIER'S LIFE

A Roman soldier's life is always hard: miles of marching, hours of guard duty, drill, sword practice and sometimes battles. If the new recruits think that's tough, wait until they meet the senior centurion!

drying socks

8 soldiers in a room

bunk beds

'gladius' swords

pilum

shield

leather sandals with iron studs

helmet and bedroll

wooden chest

pots and pans.

digging tools

vespian's sweaty men are hungry after their march.

sore feet from marching.

sore eyes from the smoke in here!

They cook together in their room.

A soldier's life was tough. Deserters could be badly beaten, or even stoned to death.

• Soldiers usually joined the army for 20 years but about half of all recruits didn't survive long enough to retire.

People have scratched silly poems and drawings on the plaster walls.

The water flows under here floating the POO away.

This is what it looks like under the floor.

• The Romans were clever plumbers – they even used lead water pipes.

• Infection and disease were common. Many Romans had roundworms from drinking dirty water and eye infections from smoky fires.

ON THE TOILET

Going to a Roman toilet is a time for a chat – no one is embarrassed or shy. A short roof keeps the rain off the seats but allows fresh air in. Running water trickles along the floor. Candidus, Vespian and Flavinus are planning an off-duty trip into town.

Fresh water flows in here.

Sponges on sticks to wipe your bum. You wash your sponge stick and put it back for someone else to use!

It's really smelly in here!

Lots of flies

There is a stone trough to wash your hands – but NO SOAP!

Next stop the bath house, the best place to be on a cold day like this!

A typical Roman toilet could seat many people at a time.

• It is possible that sponges may have been soaked in vinegar as a sort of disinfectant.

THE BATH HOUSE

The soldiers' bath house is a lovely building. It has decorated plaster walls and cold plunge pools. It has warm baths and steamy sauna rooms. It even has a changing room with board games and music – what a nice way to relax on the northern frontier!

Candidus has been on cavalry patrol for three days. He stinks like a sweaty horse!

Marcus

olive oil

voices chatting and laughing... the clacking of board games

A statue of **Fortuna**. The Roman goddess of good luck.

Romans use olive oil instead of soap. They scrape off the muck with a metal scraper called a **strigil**.

who do you think is winning?

• The bath houses and the commander's quarters were kept warm with an under-floor heating system called a hypocaust.

• Warm air from a special fire circulated under the stone floors and warmed the rooms.

It takes a lot of wood to heat the bath house.

A slave stokes the fire.

Vespian is telling Flavinus about his new puppy.

wooden sandals

Beautiful mosaic pattern

Some floors got so hot that people had to wear ooden shoes to protect their feet.

• Hollow clay bricks in the walls let the warm air circulate. The windows were double-glazed too!

Bar-Rosie
sells drinks and
tasty hot and
cold snacks.

• The settlements that grew up around every frontier fort attracted people from all over the Roman Empire.

• There were butchers, dressmakers, street musicians, magic charm sellers, wives and mothers. Retired soldiers often stayed too, opening up shops or bars.

Landlady- Mara rents out rooms to the soldiers' secret wives. She makes a lot of money.

Claudia's slave is buying all the food for the household.

Baker- Catty is a local girl. She and her daughter sell freshly baked bread.

Fishseller- Ostia has followed her sons here from far away. Her boys are both in the army.

olive stones and Roman coins.

THE — — SETTLEMENT

Over the years, a large settlement has grown outside the fort. It is where traders, shopkeepers and landladies gather to make a living from the soldiers' wages.

Only officers were allowed to marry but many soldiers had secret wives living in the settlement.

• Roman cafes opened out on to the street, selling 'fast food' like olives, honey cakes, black pudding, meatballs and barley soup. Drinks included beer and wine.

Roman Toothpaste Recipe:
Powdered horn
Ground up oyster shells
Ashes of dogs' teeth
Mixed up with honey!

Lepidina has linen underwear.

Only important Romans like Feli can wear a toga

cotton underpants

Roman children wear a lucky charm called a 'Bulla'.

slaves like Marcus do all the work.

It's hard to lace your own sandals when you're 3 years old.

• Slaves did all the work. A slave could belong to a rich owner or be shared among a group of rough soldiers. Slaves could be house-pets or worked to death!

• To keep their legs smooth and silky, Roman women used a cream made of goat's blood, mixed with sea palm and powdered snake!

DRESSING UP

Everyone is getting ready for the birthday party. The slaves are working very hard. Claudia and Lepidina take fashion very seriously. Even here, on the rainy frontier, they have copied the latest hairstyles by looking at coins and statues brought from Rome.

Roman ladies' slaves are always well dressed.

Claudia's hair smells of perfumed oil.

Lovely polished metal mirror

chalk on neck

Ochre on lips

Expensive make-up comes in glass jars.

Silk shawl from Rome

Foundation cream was made from dirt and sweat from sheep's wool. Mascara was made from bear fat and soot!

• Romans used bird droppings and honey to get rid of spots.

The slaves wait on the guests and wash their fingers between meals.

A slave goes round with a pot in case anyone needs a wee – Ugh!

PARTY

Claudia's birthday party is in the commander's quarters – the best rooms in the fort. With musicians, dancers and a magnificent feast, the celebrations will go on late into the night.

A slave brings a piglet.

Musicians play while a slave dances.

Everyone eats with their fingers.

Oil lamps light the room.

Boar's head, deer meat and chicken... Peacock eggs and frui

• A Roman party trick was to put live birds in a roast boar. They flew out when it was cut open.

• Snails were fattened up by feeding them milk or meat.

28

There is local beer too. Lots of **burping!**

Lepidina loves chicken and raw oysters.

Everyone including the children drinks watered-down wine.

chicken leg

Roman children love honey cakes!

Garlic-buttered snails.

bread

beautiful glass jug

Dormice pie!

quail eggs

Some people are sick outside so they can eat some more.

Dormice were kept in special cages and fed on nuts and acorns.

• Some Roman houses even had a special room to be sick in called the vomitorium!

ROMAN CHILDREN

Only the officers can afford a teacher at the fort. On this cold morning the boys are studying mathematics and learning that the world is flat! Girls are taught reading, writing, cooking, music and needlework at home.

Boys have to learn things 'word-for-word' – this teacher beats them with a stick if they don't remember!

statue of a famous poet

Greeks make good teachers. Max's teacher is an ex-slave.

The boys write with styli on wax tablets.

MAX

Abacus for doing sum

• Slaves could sometimes be freed as a reward for faithful service. Well-educated freed slaves often took jobs as clerks or teachers.

• Rich Romans could read and write but slaves and poor people got no education at all.

Flora likes rolling a hoop.

Titus plays with his toy chariot.

Helena is painfully out of tune. Ouch!

All boys like to play fight with wooden swords.

Balls are made from leather.

Max is clever at stick and ball games.

The Celtic tribes didn't read or write at all and they thought that Roman letters were magic spells!

• Roman children had toys like marbles, hoops, bats and balls, and model animals made of wood or leather. They also played ball games like 'catch'.

Emperor Severus is giving Candidus a crown of oak leaves for rescuing Lepidina and Titus from the ambush. This is a great honour.

THE EMPEROR

The emperor has arrived with his wife and children. They have travelled thousands of bumpy Roman miles on a tour of their frontier. The local arena is putting on a show with two famous gladiators, Paxos and Thrax.

The guard of honour wear ceremonial masks made of silver.

oak lea

• Some emperors were cruel and selfish. Others were wise. Hadrian built Hadrian's Wall and Marcus Aurelius wrote a famous book called *Meditations*.

• The most famous arena in the world was the Colosseum in Rome, but small arenas were built all over the Empire.

32

Boo! Hurrah! Boo! hiss! OOh!

She fights with a net and a trident.

He fights with a sword.

Thrax and Paxos don't fight to the death — they are too valuable! Their pretend fight is all part of the show and the crowds LOVE IT!

Paxos and Thrax give souvenirs to their fans.

At the Colosseum, unarmed prisoners were often fed to hungry lions to entertain the crowds.

• Most gladiators fought to the death and usually survived for only 2 or 3 fights.

Rosie nails a curse tablet to the temple wall. She is asking the gods to punish a thief!

Outside the temple, Felix is sacrificing a boar. He will burn the heart and the liver as offerings to Mars, god of wa[r] so his soldiers will have success in battle.

Jupiter - the king of the Roman gods...

Juno - his queen

Neptune - god of the sea

Venus - goddess of love.

Diana - goddess of the moon

Apollo - god of the sun.

Claudia's household shrine - Max leaves food as an offering to the family spirits that protect the [home]

• Little models of legs or ears made of clay or lead were left at temples to beg the gods to help heal injuries.

• All Roman families had a household shrine. The small figures represent family spirits who protect the home.

ROMAN GODS

It's dusk at the fort and all is well. The Roman gods are being worshipped tonight in this rainy place, somewhere on the northern frontier.

moths come to the light.

Vespian is wearing a raven mask.

The sweet scent of a burning pinecone fills the dark room.

Flavinus is wearing a lion head mask.

This is a secret ceremony held for Mithras, Lord of Light.

• Jupiter was father to a large family of Roman gods. His thunderbolt and eagle were the badges of Rome.

• Although gods from other religions were worshipped, Christianity wasn't popular because it didn't use sacrifices. That upset Jupiter and the emperor!

Bad news has just come in...

The frontier tribes are preparing for war!

END OF THE EMPIRE

The Roman Empire lasted hundreds of years and became Christian in AD 320. Emperor Constantine split the Empire into two, ruling the eastern part of the Empire from Constantinople in Turkey. When the western part was invaded by Germanic tribes, the legions were called home to defend Rome. But Rome was destroyed in AD 410 and the people of its once great Empire were left undefended. Many would soon face new invaders: the Saxons from Germany and the Jutes from Denmark.

WHAT THE ROMANS LEFT BEHIND . . .

Latin is still taught today and is at the heart of many modern languages like Italian and Spanish. Many Latin words exist in English, German and French too. We still use Roman letters and all the months still have Roman names. For example, March is named after Mars and June after the goddess Juno. Archaeologists have excavated buildings all over the Roman Empire, finding statues, weapons, tools, writing tablets and personal possessions. Many Roman ruins are open to visitors so why not explore a Roman fort yourself one day?

ABACUS – page 30.
A simple counting device made of wooden beads on a metal frame.
ARENA – pages 32 & 33.
A circular Roman 'sports stadium' where chariot racing, battles between gladiators and wild animal fighting could be watched.
AUXILIARIES – page 18.
Soldiers who fought for the Roman army from all corners of the Empire but who were not Roman citizens. Prisoners of war often chose to be soldiers instead of slaves.
CELTS – pages 10, 11, 14, 15 & 31.
The tribes of people living in Britain and south of Europe at the time.
CENTURY – page 8.
A unit of 80 men with its own barrack block.
CENTURION – pages 8 & 18.
An officer in charge of a century. Many started out as ordinary soldiers and so had lots of experience.
CHAIN MAIL – page 18.
Small links of iron made into a vest and worn for protection in battle.
COHORT – page 8.
An army unit made up of centuries. Usually between 500 and 1000 soldiers.
CROWN OF OAK LEAVES – page 32.
A special award given to a soldier or unit for rescuing a Roman citizen. This was also called a civica.
CURSE TABLET – page 34.
People wrote curses asking the gods to give their enemies bad luck. They left them at temples or buried them in the ground.
DECURION – page 14.
A cavalry officer.
DESERTER – page 19.
A soldier that runs away from the army.
EMPEROR – page 32 & 36.
The ruler of the Roman Empire. Rome wasn't always ruled by emperors. For hundreds of years it was ruled by a government called a Republic.
EMPIRE – pages 6, 9, 10, 11, 24 & 36.
Lands belonging to another country that have been taken in battle or invaded.

The Headquarters building is buzzing like a wasp's nest!

Vespian is doubling the guard.

GLOSSARY & INDEX